Maths
Frameworking

Intervention Workbook

Chris Pearce

Step 3 Contents

1 Number

1.1 Multiplying and dividing by 10, 100 and 1000

I can

- multiply whole numbers and decimals by 10, 100 and 1000
- divide whole numbers and decimals by 10, 100 and 1000

Example

Work out the following:

a 5.7×100 **b** $570 \div 1000$

Solution

a Write 5.7 in columns headed units (U), tens (T), hundreds (H), tenths (t), and so on.

It is easier to do this neatly on square paper.

To multiply by 100, move each digit two places to the left.

Th	H	T	U ·	t	h	th
			· 5 · 7			
	5	7	·			

The answer is 570.

You must put a 0 in the units column.

b Write 570 in columns. To divide by 1000, move each digit three places to the left.

Th	H	T	U ·	t	h	th
	5	7	0 ·			
			· 5	7	0	

The answer is 0.57.

You do not need a 0 in the thousandths column.

Practice questions

1 Multiply these numbers by 10.

a 7 _____

b 7.4 _____

c 7.9 _____

d 66 _____

e 6.6 _____

f 0.66 _____

g 40 _____

h 0.45 _____

i 9.87 _____

j 0.023 _____

k 807 _____

l 6.052 _____

2 Divide these numbers by 10.

a 5 _____

b 5.2 _____

c 5.4 _____

d 28 _____

e 2.8 _____

f 0.28 _____

g 0.9 _____

h 800 _____

i 20.99 _____

j 0.03 _____

k 569 _____

l 75.63 _____

3 Multiply these numbers by 100.

a 3 _____

b 3.1 _____

c 3.14 _____

d 90 _____

e 2 _____

f 9.25 _____

g 0.54 _____

h 290 _____

i 0.025 _____

j 7.654 _____

k 30.5 _____

l 1.26 _____

4 Divide these numbers by 100.

a 400 _____

b 430 _____

c 438 _____

d 60 _____

e 69 _____

f 5 _____

g 0.3 _____

h 8.7 _____

i 42.3 _____

j 90.2 _____

k 8000 _____

l 6250 _____

5 Multiply these numbers by 1000.

a 4 _____

b 4.4 _____

c 44 _____

d 0.44 _____

e 6.7 _____

f 3.75 _____

g 0.5 _____

h 2.64 _____

i 0.075 _____

j 0.106 _____

k 17.2 _____

l 4.93 _____

6 Divide these numbers by 1000.

a 7000 _____

b 7300 _____

c 7125 _____

d 350 _____

e 35 _____

f 8 _____

g 505 _____

h 8040 _____

i 3.5 _____

j 0.9 _____

k 7800 _____

l 69.2 _____

7 Fill in each of the missing numbers using 10, 100 or 1000.

a $3.8 \times$ _____ $= 38$

b $0.65 \times$ _____ $= 650$

c $7.45 \times$ _____ $= 7450$

d $15 \times$ _____ $= 1500$

e $0.03 \times$ _____ $= 30$

f $1.03 \times$ _____ $= 103$

8 Fill in each of the missing numbers using 10, 100 or 1000.

a $45 \div$ _____ $= 0.45$

b $320 \div$ _____ $= 0.32$

c $5460 \div$ _____ $= 546$

d $7.9 \div$ _____ $= 0.79$

e $15 \div$ _____ $= 0.15$

f $303 \div$ _____ $= 0.303$

3 Work out these percentages without a calculator.

  a 50% of £13 = _____

  b 25% of 60 g = _____

  c 20% of 35 km = _____

  d 75% of 14 = _____

  e 80% of 50 = _____

  f 30% of 400 = _____

  g 30% of £6.00 = _____

  h 70% of 120 m = _____

  i 90% of £3.10 = _____

  j 30% of £3.30 = _____

4 Work out these percentages. You can use a calculator.

  a 23% of £16.00 = _____

  b 42% of 65 = _____

  c 86% of 24 m = _____

  d 9% of £67 = _____

  e 17% of 17 kg = _____

  f 4% of 7900 = _____

  g 72% of 8.5 g = _____

  h 36% of 7300 people = _____

  i 2.5% of £3000 = _____

  j 6.5% of £370 = _____

  k 44% of 680 = _____

  l 39% of 6.2 km = _____

1.7 Calculations without a calculator

I can

- multiply a three-digit number by a two-digit number
- divide a three-digit number by a two-digit number

Example

Work out the following:

a 383×17 **b** $383 \div 17$

Solution

a You could use the column method or the grid method.

```
    3 8 3
  x   1 7
  3 8 3 0
  2 6 8 1
    5 2
  6 5 1 1
  1 1
```

or

	300	80	3
10	3000	800	30
7	2100	560	21

```
  3 0 0 0
    8 0 0
      3 0
  2 1 0 0
    5 6 0
+     2 1
  6 5 1 1
  1 1
```

The answer is 6511.

b You could set out the division like this.

```
       2 2 r 9
  17)3 8⁴3
```

17 does not go into 3.

17 goes into 38 twice, because $17 \times 2 = 34$.

The remainder is 4.

17 goes into 43 twice with a remainder of 9.

The answer is 22 remainder 9.

Practice questions

Do not use a calculator for these questions. Show your working.

1 Work out these multiplications.

     a $142 \times 32 =$ _____   **b** $163 \times 15 =$ _____   **c** $309 \times 45 =$ _____

d $427 \times 33 =$ _____

e $530 \times 18 =$ _____

f $612 \times 71 =$ _____

g $23 \times 254 =$ _____

h $52 \times 381 =$ _____

i $802 \times 19 =$ _____

2 Work out these divisions.

a $325 \div 13 =$ _____

b $602 \div 14 =$ _____

c $960 \div 15 =$ _____

d $851 \div 23 =$ _____

e $930 \div 21 =$ _____

f $840 \div 32 =$ _____

g $720 \div 54 =$ _____

h $900 \div 16 =$ _____

i $666 \div 41 =$ _____

1.8 Negative numbers

I can

- put negative numbers in order
- add and subtract negative numbers

Example

Work out the following:

a $-3 + 5$ **b** $-3 - 5$ **c** $-3 + -5$ **d** $-3 - -5$

Solution

a A number line can be useful.

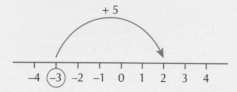

To add 5 to −3, move 5 to the *right*. $-3 + 5 = 2$

b

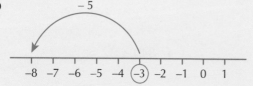

To subtract 5 from −3, move 5 to the *left*. $-3 - 5 = -8$

c To add a negative number (−5), subtract the inverse (5). The diagram is the same as part b.
$-3 + -5 = -3 - 5 = -8$

d To subtract a negative number (−5), add the inverse (5). The diagram is the same as part a.
$-3 - -5 = -3 + 5 = 2$

Practice questions

1   Write these numbers in order, from smallest to largest.

8   −10   7   −3   0   −5   _____

2 Here are some metric units.

g   m   l   kg   km   mg   ml

Choose the most suitable unit to measure

a the capacity of a spoon _____

b the mass of a dog _____

c the height of a building _____

d the quantity of water in a swimming pool _____

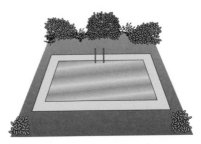

e the amount of salt used in a recipe _____

3 Change these lengths to metres.

a 200 cm = _____ m   **b** 3 km = _____ m   **c** 5000 mm = _____ m

4 Change these lengths to centimetres.

a 2.5 m = _____ cm   **b** 340 mm = _____ cm   **c** 7 mm = _____ cm

5 Draw a line between the two capacities that are the same. Circle the odd one out.

6 Convert these masses into grams.

a 4 kg = _____ g

b 1.3 kg = _____ g

c 0.25 kg = _____ g

d 9.5 kg = _____ g

e 2000 mg = _____ g

f 500 mg = _____ g

7 Convert these units.

a 300 mm = _____ cm

b 300 cm = _____ m

c 300 m = _____ km

d 4250 g = _____ kg

e 0.4 kg = _____ g

f 6500 mg = _____ g

g 2.5 l = _____ ml

h 100 ml = _____ l

i 350 ml = _____ l

1.11 Number relationships

I can

• work out common factors and common multiples

Example

a Find all the common factors of 12 and 15.

b Find two common multiples of 12 and 15.

Solution

a $12 = 1 \times 12$

$12 = 2 \times 6$ *The factors of 12 are 1, 2, 3, 4, 6 and 12.*

$12 = 3 \times 4$

$15 = 1 \times 15$
    The factors of 15 are 1, 3, 5 and 15.
$15 = 3 \times 5$

The **common factors** are factors of *both* numbers. They are 1 and 3.

b The multiples of 12 are 12, 24, 36, 48, 60, 72, …

The multiples of 15 are 15, 30, 45, 60, 75, …

The **common multiples** are the numbers in *both* lists.

The first common multiple is 60. Further common multiples are 120, 180, 240, and so on.

Practice questions

1   **a** Work out the factors of 16.   _____

     b Work out the factors of 28.   _____

     c Write down the common factors of 16 and 28.   _____

2   **a** Work out the factors of 18.   _____

     b Work out the factors of 27.   _____

     c Write down the common factors of 18 and 27.   _____

3 **a** Work out the factors of 45.

_____

    b Work out the factors of 63.

_____

    c Write down the common factors of 45 and 63.

_____

4 Work out the common factors of 30 and 40.

_____

5 Work out the common factors of 50 and 75.

_____

6 **a** Write down the first six multiples of 3.

_____

    b Write down the first six multiples of 5.

_____

    c Work out two common multiples of 3 and 5.

_____

7 **a** Write down the first five multiples of 10.

_____

    b Write down the first five multiples of 15.

_____

    c Work out three common multiples of 10 and 15.

_____

8 Work out two common multiples of 20 and 25.

_____

9 Work out two common multiples of 9 and 12.

_____

1.12 Number patterns

I can

• recognise number patterns

Example

Here is a sequence of numbers.   1   2   4   7   11   16

Work out the next two numbers in the sequence.

Solution

Look at the differences between the numbers.

The differences increase by one each time.

The next number is 16 + 6 = 22.

Then the one after that is 22 + 7 = 29.

Practice questions

1   Work out the next two numbers in each of these sequences.

a 17   20   23   26   29   32   _____   _____

b 3   4   6   9   13   18   _____   _____

c 10   12   16   22   30   40   _____   _____

d 1   2   5   10   17   _____   _____

e 80   76   72   68   _____   _____

f 50   49   47   44   40   _____   _____

g 3   4   7   12   19   28   _____   _____

h 9   9.5   11   13.5   17   21.5   _____   _____

2 Here is a sequence of patterns.

1 + 2 = 3   1 + 2 + 3 = 6   1 + 2 + 3 + 4 = 10

Work out the next two sums in the sequence.

_____

3 Here is a different sequence of patterns.

1 + 3 = 4   1 + 3 + 5 = 9   1 + 3 + 5 + 7 = 16

Work out the next two sums in the sequence.

_____

4 Fill in the missing numbers in these sequences.

    a   9   14   19   _____   29   _____   _____   44

    b 40   37   34   31   _____   _____   _____   19

    c   4   5   7   10   _____   19   _____   32   _____

    d   1   2   5   10   _____   26   37   _____   65

1.13 Squares, cubes and roots

I can

- work out the square or the cube of a number
- work out the square root or the cube root of a number

Example

Work out

a 5^2 **b** 5^3 **c** $\sqrt{64}$ **d** $\sqrt[3]{64}$

Solution

a 5^2 is '5 squared'. $5^2 = 5 \times 5 = 25$

b 5^3 is '5 cubed'. $5^3 = 5 \times 5 \times 5 = 125$

c $\sqrt{64}$ is the square root of 64. $8^2 = 8 \times 8 = 64$ so $\sqrt{64} = 8$

d $\sqrt[3]{64}$ is the cube root of 64. $4^3 = 4 \times 4 \times 4 = 64$ so $\sqrt[3]{64} = 4$

Practice questions

Do not use a calculator for these questions.

1   Work out

   a $3^2 = $ _____   **b** $6^2 = $ _____   **c** $9^2 = $ _____   **d** $12^2 = $ _____

2   Work out

   a $2^3 = $ _____   **b** $3^3 = $ _____   **c** $6^3 = $ _____   **d** $10^3 = $ _____

3   Work out

   a $1^2 + 2^2 = $ _____   **b** $3^2 + 4^2 = $ _____

   c $8^2 + 10^2 = $ _____   **d** $15^2 + 20^2 = $ _____

4 Work out

a $3^2 - 2^3 =$ _____

b $3^3 - 5^2 =$ _____

c $5^3 - 4^3 =$ _____

d $10^3 - 10^2 =$ _____

5 Work out

a $\sqrt{9} =$ _____

b $\sqrt{49} =$ _____

c $\sqrt{81} =$ _____

d $\sqrt{121} =$ _____

e $\sqrt{100} =$ _____

f $\sqrt{1} =$ _____

g $\sqrt{196} =$ _____

h $\sqrt{400} =$ _____

i $\sqrt{0} =$ _____

6 Work out

a $\sqrt[3]{1} =$ _____

b $\sqrt[3]{8} =$ _____

c $\sqrt[3]{125} =$ _____

d $\sqrt[3]{1000} =$ _____

e $\sqrt[3]{216} =$ _____

f $\sqrt[3]{729} =$ _____

7 Fill in the missing numbers.

a _____$^2 = 36$ **b** _____$^2 = 100$ **c** _____$^3 = 27$ **d** _____$^3 = 64$

8 Fill in the missing numbers.

a $\sqrt{\underline{\quad}} = 5$ **b** $\sqrt{\underline{\quad}} = 9$ **c** $\sqrt[3]{\underline{\quad}} = 4$ **d** $\sqrt[3]{\underline{\quad}} = 6$

Comments, next steps, misconceptions

2 Algebra

2.1 Formulae

I can

- use and construct simple formulae

Example

A plumber has a call-out charge of £40 and then charges £32 an hour for the work done.

If he works for n hours, the total cost, £c, is given by the formula $c = 40 + 32n$.

a Work out the total cost if a job takes 2.5 hours.

b The plumber decides to increase the hourly charge to £34. Write down a new formula for the total cost.

Solution

a If $n = 2.5$, then $c = 40 + 32 \times 2.5 = 40 + 80 = 120$.

The total cost is £120.

b Replace 32 in the formula by 34.

The new formula is $c = 40 + 34n$.

Practice questions

1 Tom is 3 years older than Emma. The formula for working out Tom's age is:

$T = E + 3$ where T = Tom's age

E = Emma's age

a Use the formula to work out Tom's age when Emma's age is

i 20 years _____   **ii** 49 years _____   **iii** 72 years _____

b Jamie is 8 years younger than Emma. J = Jamie's age

Complete the formula for Jamie's age in terms of Emma's age. $J =$ _____

2 A driving instructor works 6.5 hours every day. He uses this formula to work out how long he works:

$h = 6.5d$ where h = the total number of hours he works

d = the number of days he works

a Use the formula to work out the number of hours he works in

i 2 days _____   **ii** 4 days _____   **iii** 10 days _____

b The driving instructor reduces the number of hours per day to 5.5 hours.

Complete his new formula for h. $h =$ _____

3 A café orders eggs in boxes of six.

The formula for working out the total number of eggs delivered is:

$E = 6N$ where E = number of eggs

N = number of boxes

a Use the formula to work out the number of eggs if the café orders

i 6 boxes _____   **ii** 10 boxes _____   **iii** 30 boxes _____

b In future the eggs will be delivered in boxes of ten.

Complete a new formula for E. $E =$ _____

4 A taxi driver charges £2.50 for each kilometre of a journey. She uses this formula to work out the total cost of a taxi fare:

$f = 2.5m + 3$ where f = fare in pounds

m = number of kilometres travelled

a Use the formula to work out the fare for a journey of

i 4 km _____   **ii** 8 km _____   **iii** 20 km _____

b The cost for each kilometre is increased to £2.80.

Work out a new formula for the fare. _____

5

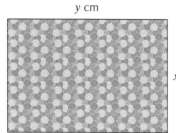

y cm

x cm

a Write down a formula for the perimeter, p cm, of this rectangle in terms of x and y.

_____

b Find the value of p if x = 20 and y = 30. _____

c Write down a formula for the area, a cm², of this rectangle in terms of x and y.

_____

d Find the value of a if x = 20 and y = 30. _____

6 Write down a formula for the perimeter, p, of each of the following shapes as simply as possible.

a

3a   3a

a

_____

b

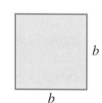

b

b

_____

c

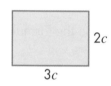

2c

3c

_____

d

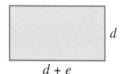

d

d + e

_____

e

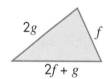

2g   f

2f + g

_____

7 The formula for the area, a cm², of this triangle is a = 0.35pq.

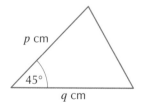

p cm

45°

q cm

Use the formula to work out the area of the triangle if p = 5 and

q = 6. _____

2.2 Coordinates

I can

• use and interpret coordinates in all four quadrants

Example

a Plot the points A (3,–4), B (–3, 2), C (–1,–4) and D (5,–2) on a grid.

b Join the four points to make a square.

c Work out the coordinates of the centre of the square.

Solution

a and b The first number is the *x*-coordinate (horizontal) and the second number is the *y*-coordinate (vertical).

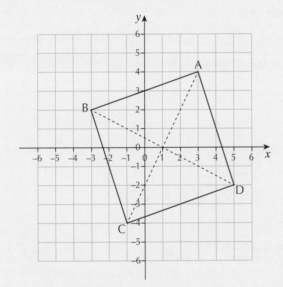

c Draw in the diagonals. They cross in the centre of the square.

The centre has coordinates (1, 0).

Practice questions

1 Here are the coordinates of points on the grid. Write the letter of the point next to each pair of coordinates.

a (–4, –2) _____

b (2, 2) _____

c (–2, –4) _____

d (3, –2) _____

e (4, 0) _____

f (–2, 4) _____

g (0, –3) _____

h (3, 5) _____

i (2, –5) _____

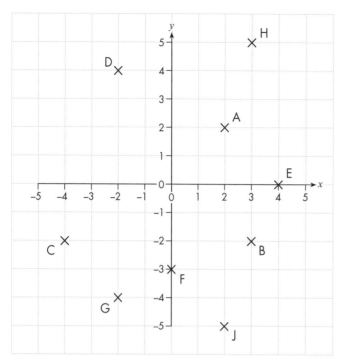

2 Plot the following points on the grid. Join the points with a ruler as you plot them.

(2, 4) (4, 2) (4, −1) (2, −3) (−1, −3) (−3, −1) (−3, 2) (−1, 4) (2, 4)

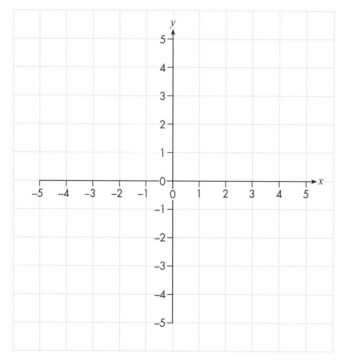

Name the shape you have drawn. _____

3 Each set of coordinates below gives three of the four corners of a rectangle.

On squared paper, draw a coordinate grid for each set (from −6 to +6 on both axes), plot the points and join them with a ruler. Complete the rectangle and write down the coordinates of the fourth corner.

a (−3, 3) (5, 3) (5,−2) _____   **b** (−2, 2) (1, 5) (3, 3) _____

4 Draw a coordinate grid from −6 to 6 on both axes and plot each set of points, joining them to form a straight line.

a (4, 5) (2, 3) (0, 1) (−3,−2) (−5,−4)

What do you notice about the coordinates?

_____

b (−3,−6) (−1,−4) (1,−2) (3,0) (6,3)

What do you notice about the coordinates?

_____

Comments, next steps, misconceptions

3 Ratio, proportion and rates of change

3.1 Ratio

I can

* understand and use simple ratios

Example

Here are the prices of some new cars.

Aztec	£16 000
Inca	£24 000
Maya	£32 000

Work out, as simply as possible, the ratios of these prices.

a Aztec to Maya **b** Inca to Aztec **c** Maya to Inca

Solution

a The ratio of the prices is 16000 : 32000.   *Notice that we write the Aztec first.*

Look for a common factor to divide by.

Divide both numbers by 1000 to get 16 : 32.

Divide both numbers by 16 to get 1 : 2.

b The ratio is 24000 : 16000 = 24 : 16.

Divide both of these numbers by 8 to get 3 : 2.

You could have divided by 2 to get 12 : 8 and then by 4 to get 3 : 2. The answer is the same.

c The ratio is 32000 : 24000 = 32 : 24.

Divide by 8 this time to get 4 : 3. *It cannot be simplified any more.*

Practice questions

1 A cake recipe uses these ingredients.

Flour	200 g
Sugar	50 g
Butter	100 g
Chocolate	25 g

Work out these ratios. Write the ratios as simply as possible.

a mass of flour to mass of butter   _____

b mass of sugar to mass of flour   _____

c mass of flour to mass of chocolate   _____

2 Write each ratio in its simplest form.

a 3 : 6 = _____   **b** 10 : 5 = _____   **c** 6 : 6 = _____

d 60 : 20 = _____   **e** 100 : 150 = _____   **f** 80 : 4 = _____

g 100 : 2 = _____   **h** 9 : 45 = _____   **i** 160 : 40 = _____

j 300 : 120 = _____   **k** 60 : 90 = _____   **l** 150 : 25 = _____

3

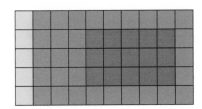

Write these ratios as simply as possible.

a yellow squares to blue squares = _____   **b** red squares to yellow squares = _____

c green squares to blue squares = _____   **d** red squares to blue squares = _____

4 There are 10 girls and 15 boys in class 9B.

Write the ratio of **girls to boys** in its simplest form. _____

5 There are 30 boys and 90 girls in a hall.

Write the ratio of **boys to girls** in its simplest form. _____

6 There are 72 men and 18 women in a sports club.

Write the ratio of **men to women** in its simplest form. _____

7 There are 60 vehicles in a car park. Five are vans. The rest are cars.

Write the ratio of **cars to vans** in its simplest form. _____

8 Here are the costs of some new cars.

Supreme	£16 000
Arrow	£24 000
Indian	£40 000
Domino	£80 000

Work out the ratios of these prices. Write your answers as simply as possible.

a Domino to Supreme _____   **b** Indian to Arrow _____

3.2 Proportion

I can

- solve simple problems involving ratio and proportion

20 litres of petrol cost £26.40. Find the cost of 60 litres.

Solution

Here are two ways to answer the question.

Method 1

20 litres cost £26.40 so one litre costs £26.40 ÷ 20 = 1.32.

60 litres cost £1.32 × 60 = £79.20.

Method 2

The ratio of 60 litres to 20 litres is 60 : 20 = 3 : 1.   *Divide both numbers by 60.*

The cost of 60 litres = 3 × the cost of 20 litres

= 3 × £26.40

= £79.20.

Practice questions

1   The cost of 4 kg of potatoes is £3.76.

Work out the cost of 12 kg. _____

2   The cost of six oranges is £2.58.

Work out the cost of 24 oranges. _____

3   The cost of five tickets for a concert is £76.25.

Work out the cost of 40 tickets. _____

4   A car travels 23 miles in 30 minutes.

If it travels at the same speed, how far will it travel in 3 hours? _____

5   A jogger takes 15 minutes to jog 1.8 miles.

If she jogs at the same speed, how far
will she jog in one hour?

_____

6   15 grams of gold cost £351.

Work out the cost of 5 grams of gold. _____

7   A postman delivers 30 letters in 20 minutes.

If he continues at the same rate, how long will he take to deliver 120 letters?

_____

8   The cost of 24 stamps for standard letters is £11.52.

Work out the cost of six stamps. _____

9   The cost of 75 litres of diesel fuel is £110.25.

Work out the cost of 25 litres. _____

10   Complete this table showing the cost of fence panels

Number of panels	3	6	12	18	24
Cost		£141			

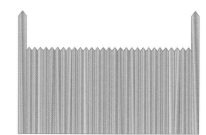

Comments, next steps, misconceptions

4 Geometry and measures

4.1 Symmetry

I can

- identify reflection symmetry in 2D shapes
- identify rotation symmetry in 2D shapes

Example

a i How many lines of symmetry does this shape have?

  ii Colour two squares so that it has four lines of symmetry.

b i What is the order of rotational symmetry of this shape?

  ii Colour two squares so that it has rotational symmetry of order four.

Solution

a i It has two lines of symmetry. They pass through opposite corners.

  ii Colour the other two corners. This will make the shape symmetrical horizontally and vertically as well as diagonally.

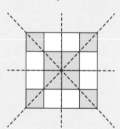

The four lines of symmetry have been drawn on the shape.

b i It has rotational symmetry of order two.

  ii Colour the two squares as shown.

The shape now has rotational symmetry of order four. If you rotate the shape about the centre it will come back on itself four times in one complete revolution. You can check this with tracing paper.

Practice questions

1 All of these shapes have line symmetry. Draw the lines of symmetry on each shape.

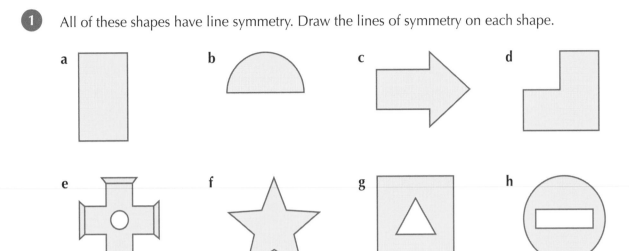

2 Some of these shapes do not have line symmetry. Put a tick inside the shapes that have line symmetry. Put a cross inside those that do not.

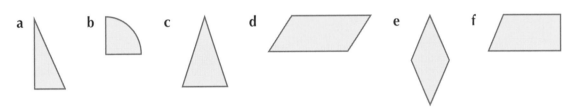

3 If possible, add one extra square to give the shape

a four lines of symmetry.

b one line of symmetry.

c no lines of symmetry.

Say if it is not possible.

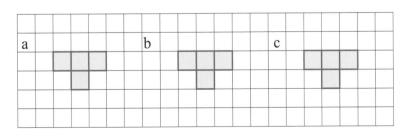

4 **a** Shade in squares to turn the dashed line into a line of symmetry.

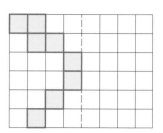

b Shade in squares to turn both the dashed lines into lines of symmetry.

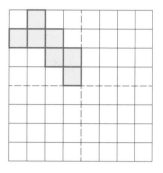

5 Work out the order of rotation symmetry of each shape.

a

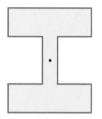

Order _____

b

Order _____

c

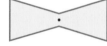

Order _____

d

Order _____

e

Order _____

f

Order _____

6 Some shapes do not have rotation symmetry.

Put a 1 inside shapes that do **not** have rotation symmetry.

Write the order of rotation symmetry inside the other shapes.

a 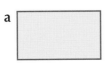   b 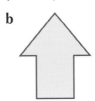   c   d

e    f 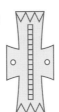   g

7 Write down the order of rotation symmetry of each design.

a 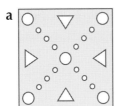   b   c   d   e

Order _____   Order _____   Order _____   Order _____   Order _____

8 Complete these shapes so they have rotation symmetry of the given order about the centre shown.

a    b   c   d

Order 2   Order 4   Order 3   Order 2

4.2 3D shapes

I can

* identify properties of 3D shapes

Example

This is a square-based pyramid.

Work out the number of

a faces   **b** edges   **c** vertices

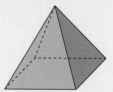

Solution

a There is a square base and four triangular faces. There are five faces all together.

b Two faces meet at an edge. There are four edges round the base and four sloping edges. There are eight edges all together.

c There is a vertex at each end of an edge. There are four vertices round the base and one more at the top. There are five vertices all together.

Practice questions

1 This is a cube.

Write down the number of

a faces _____   **b** edges _____   **c** vertices _____

2 The shape of this wooden block is a triangular prism.

Work out the number of

a faces _____   **b** edges _____   **c** vertices _____

3 This shape is an octahedron.

It has eight triangular faces.

a How many vertices does it have? _____

b How many edges does it have? _____

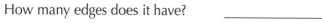

4 A prism is sliced into three parts.

  a Look at the yellow slice. Complete this sentence.

  The yellow slice has _____ edges and _____ vertices.

  b Two of the faces of the yellow slice are squares.

  What shape are the other faces? _____.

5 All these shapes are hexagonal prisms.

A hexagonal prism has eight faces. Two are hexagons. The other six are rectangles.

  a How many vertices does a hexagonal prism have? _____

  b How many edges does a hexagonal prism have? _____

6 Four cubes are balanced one on top of the other.

  a How many square faces are completely visible? _____

  b How many square faces are not completely visible? _____

7 A pyramid is placed on top of a cube to make this shape.

For this shape, work out the number of

  a vertices _____   **b** faces _____   **c** edges _____

4.3 Measuring angles

I can

- use a protractor to measure angles of any size

Example

a Draw this triangle.

b Measure angle C.

c Measure the length of BC.

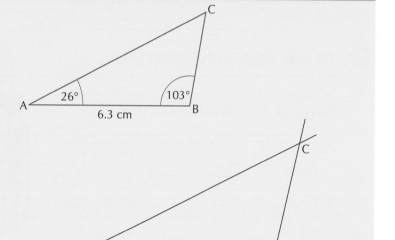

Solution

a Start by drawing AB.

Draw the angles at A and B.

The lines cross at C.

b Angle C is 51°.

c The length of BC is 3.5 or 3.6 cm.

Practice questions

1 Use a ruler and a protractor to make an accurate drawing of each of the following triangles. Measure and label the third angle.

a

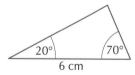

b

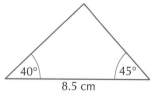

c

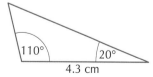

d

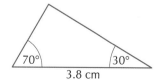

2 Use a ruler and a protractor to make an accurate drawing of each of the following triangles. Measure and label the other angles on your drawing.

a

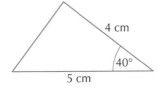

4 cm
40°
5 cm

b

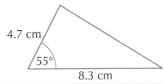

4.7 cm
55°
8.3 cm

c

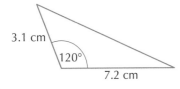

3.1 cm
120°
7.2 cm

d

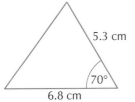

5.3 cm
70°
6.8 cm

3 Construct each of the following triangles accurately on squared paper. Remember to label all of the lines and angles. Measure the lines shown.

a

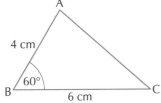

A
4 cm
60°
B   6 cm   C

AC = _____ cm

b

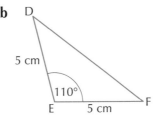

D
5 cm
110°
E   5 cm   F

DF = _____ cm

c

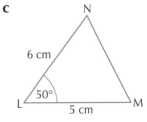

N
6 cm
50°
L   5 cm   M

NM = _____ cm

d

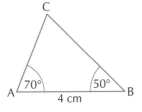

C
70°   50°
A   4 cm   B

CB = _____ cm

e

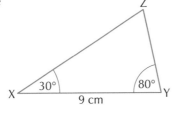

Z
30°   80°
X   9 cm   Y

XZ = _____ cm

f

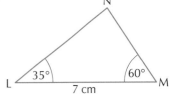

N
35°   60°
L   7 cm   M

LN = _____ cm

4.4 Calculating angles

I can

- work out angles of a triangle
- work out angles round a point

Practice questions

1 Find the missing angles.

$a = $ _____ °

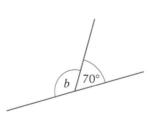

$b = $ _____ °

$c = $ _____ °

$d = $ _____ °

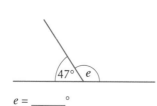

$e = $ _____ °

$f = $ _____ °

2 Find the missing angles.

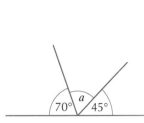

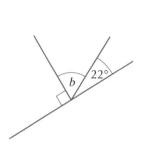

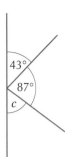

$a =$ _____ °

$b =$ _____ °

$c =$ _____ °

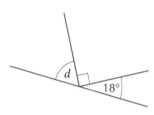

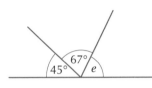

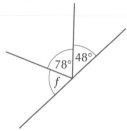

$d =$ _____ °

$e =$ _____ °

$f =$ _____ °

3 Find the missing angles.

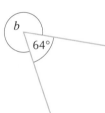

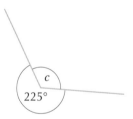

$a =$ _____ °

$b =$ _____ °

$c =$ _____ °

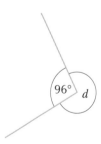

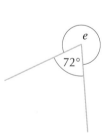

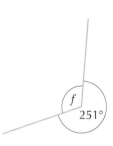

$d =$ _____ °

$e =$ _____ °

$f =$ _____ °

4 Find the missing angles.

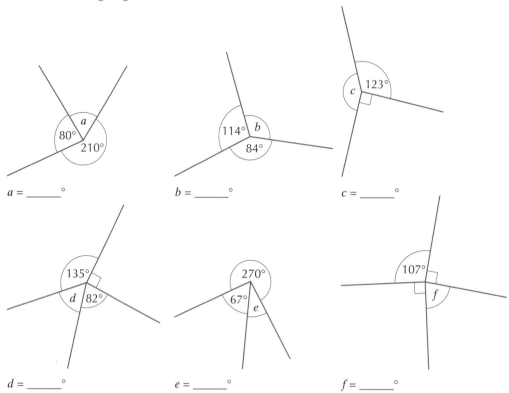

$a =$ _____ °

$b =$ _____ °

$c =$ _____ °

$d =$ _____ °

$e =$ _____ °

$f =$ _____ °

5 Find the size of the angle marked by a letter in each triangle.

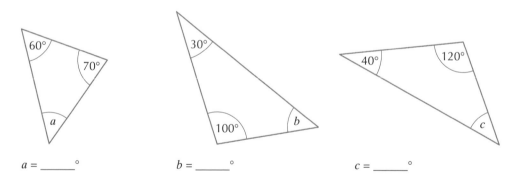

$a =$ _____ °

$b =$ _____ °

$c =$ _____ °

6 Find the size of the unknown angles in each isosceles triangle.

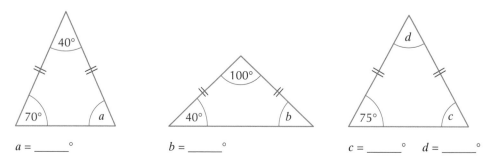

$a =$ _____ °

$b =$ _____ °

$c =$ _____ ° $d =$ _____ °

4.5 Area and perimeter

I can

- use the formula for the area of a rectangle
- distinguish between area and perimeter

Example

This is the plan of the floor of a room.

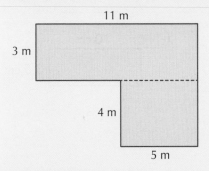

a Work out the area of the floor.

b Work out the perimeter of the floor.

Solution

a There are two rectangles.

The area of the top rectangle is $3 \times 11 = 33$ m².

The area of the bottom rectangle is $4 \times 5 = 20$ m².

The total area is $33 + 20 = 53$ m².

The sides are in metres (m) so the area is in square metres (m²).

b There are two missing lengths.

The right-hand side is $3 + 4 = 7$ m.

The other missing length is $11 - 5 = 6$ m.

The perimeter is the total length round the edge of the room.

The perimeter is $11 + 7 + 5 + 4 + 6 + 3 = 36$ m.

The sides are in metres so the perimeter is in metres.

Practice questions

1 Work out the area of each rectangle using the formula $A = l \times w$.

a   7 cm
⬜ 3 cm

A = _____ cm²

b   5 cm
 5 cm

A = _____ cm²

c   6 cm
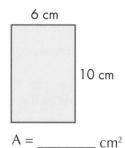 10 cm

A = _____ cm²

d   8 cm
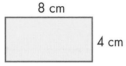 4 cm

A = _____ cm²

e   3 cm
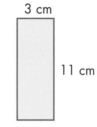 11 cm

A = _____ cm²

f   10 cm
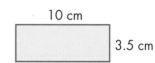 3.5 cm

A = _____ cm²

2 Work out the perimeter of each rectangle in Question 1.

a _____

b _____

c _____

d _____

e _____

f _____

3 The table shows the length and width of five rectangles.

Work out the area of each rectangle.

Length	Width	Area
7 cm	11 cm	
4 m	15 m	
10 cm	25 cm	
13 km	4 km	
12 cm	32 cm	

4 These shapes have been divided into rectangles.

Work out the area of each rectangle, then find the total area of the shape.

a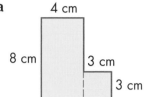

Area = _____ cm²

b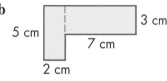

Area = _____ cm²

c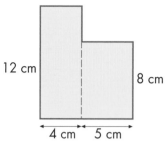

Area = _____ cm²

5 Work out the perimeter of each shape in Question 4.

a _____

b _____

c _____

6 Find the unknown length or width for each rectangle.

a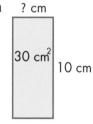

_____ cm

b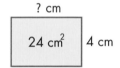

_____ cm

c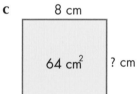

_____ cm

d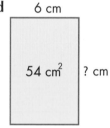

_____ cm

Comments, next steps, misconceptions

4 Geometry and measures

5 Probability

5.1 Probability scales

I can

- understand and use a probability scale

The probability of rain tomorrow is 25%.

The probability of snow in January is $\frac{4}{5}$.

Here are six events marked on a probability scale.

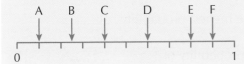

a Which one is 'It will rain tomorrow'?

b Which one is 'It will snow in January'?

Solution

a The probability it will rain tomorrow is 25% which is the same as $\frac{1}{4}$.

B is a quarter of the way along the probability line from 0 to 1, so the answer is B.

b The probability line is marked off in tenths. $\frac{4}{5} = \frac{8}{10} = 0.8$, so the answer is E because that points to 0.8.

Practice questions

1. Draw arrows on the probability scale to indicate the likelihood of each of these events. The first one has been done for you.

a It will snow in December.

b Someone in your class will arrive late for school today.

c You will live to be 300 years old.

d The next baby born will be a boy.

e The next person to come into the room will be left-handed.

f The sun will rise tomorrow.

g You will catch a cold this year.

2 This probability scale has five outcomes marked on it. They are labelled from A to E.

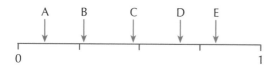

Write down the letter of the outcome that has

a the lowest probability _____

b the highest probability _____

c a probability close to 50% _____

d a probability of $\frac{2}{3}$ _____

3 Here are eight outcomes on a probability scale.

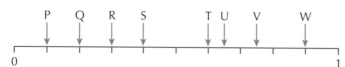

Write down the letter of the outcome with a probability of

a 30% _____

b $\frac{3}{4}$ _____

c 60% _____

d $\frac{1}{5}$ _____

e $\frac{9}{10}$ _____

f 0.4 _____

4 Work out the probability of each outcome, giving your answer as a fraction. Draw an arrow to show its position on the probability scale.

```
├────────┬────────┬────────┬────────┤
0        1        1        3        1
         ─        ─        ─
         4        2        4
```

a A flipped coin landing on Heads = _____

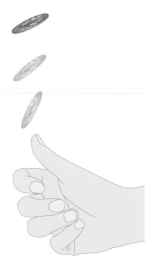

b A rolled dice landing on 7 = _____

c Getting a 3 on this spinner = _____

d A rolled dice landing on a number from 1 to 6 = _____

e Getting an even number on this spinner = _____

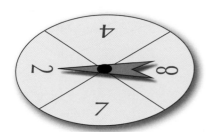

5.2 Equally likely outcomes

I can

- work out probabilities based on equally likely outcomes

Example

This dice has ten faces, numbered from 0 to 9.

The dice is rolled. What is the probability of getting

a 3? **b** a multiple of 3? **c** more than 3?

Solution

a There are ten faces and they are all equally likely.

The probability of a 3 is $\frac{1}{10}$. *You could write this as 0.1 or as 10%.*

b The multiples of 3 on the dice are 3, 6 and 9.

There are three of these, so the probability is $\frac{3}{10}$. *You could write this as 0.3 or as 30%.*

c The numbers greater than 3 on the dice are 4, 5, 6, 7, 8 or 9.

There are six of these, so the probability is $\frac{6}{10} = \frac{3}{5}$. *You could write this as 0.6 or as 60%.*

Practice questions

1 A bag contains three red counters and four green counters.

   a The probability of picking a green counter = _____

   b The probability of picking a red counter = _____

2 A box of plastic shapes contains three triangles and seven stars.

   a The probability of picking a star = _____

   b The probability of picking a triangle = _____

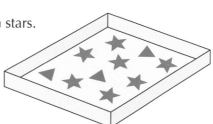

3 This spinner can land on 1 or 2.

   a The probability of landing on 1 = _____

   b The probability of landing on 2 = _____

4 A bag contains one yellow, two red and two green counters.

  a The probability of picking a green counter = _____

  b The probability of picking a counter that is not green = _____

5 This spinner can land on the numbers 1 to 8.

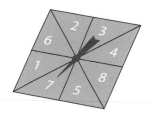

  a The probability of landing on 7 = _____

  b The probability of not landing on 7 = _____

6 **a** What is the probability that a flipped coin lands on Heads? _____

  b What is the probability that a flipped coin lands on Tails? _____

7 **a** What is the probability of getting a 3 on

  a normal dice? _____

  b What is the probability of getting an odd

  number on a normal dice? _____

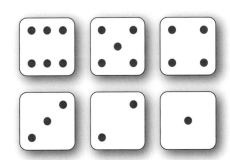

8 There are 5 red and 15 white counters in a bag.

  a What is the probability of taking a red counter at random from the bag? _____

  b What is the probability of taking a white counter at random from the bag? _____

9 A card is taken at random from these cards.

  a What is the probability that the card is the letter B? _____

  b What is the probability that the card is a vowel? _____

  c What is the probability that the card is a consonant? _____

10 In a raffle 100 tickets are sold. Jos has 5 tickets.

What is the probability that Jos wins the prize? _____

Comments, next steps, misconceptions

⬤ ⬤ ⬤

☐ ☐ ☐

☐ ☐ ☐

☐ ☐ ☐

☐ ☐ ☐

☐ ☐ ☐

☐ ☐ ☐

☐ ☐ ☐

☐ ☐ ☐

☐ ☐ ☐

☐ ☐ ☐

☐ ☐ ☐

☐ ☐ ☐

☐ ☐ ☐

☐ ☐ ☐

☐ ☐ ☐

☐ ☐ ☐

6 Statistics

6.1 Statistical measures

I can

- calculate the mean, mode and median of a set of data
- use the mean, mode or median to describe a distribution
- calculate the range of a set of data

Example

This frequency table shows the ages of 20 teenagers.

Age	13	14	15	16
Frequency	9	6	3	2

Work out

a the modal age   **b** the median age   **c** the mean age   **d** the range

Solution

a The mode is the most common. This is the age with the highest frequency.

There are nine teenagers who are 13 years old. 13 is the modal age.

b Here are the 20 ages in a list.

13   13   13   13   13   13   13   13   13   14   ↓   14   14

14   14   14   15   15   15   16   16

The median is in the middle of the list, halfway between the 10th and 11th ages. It is marked with an arrow.

The median age is 14 years.

c The mean is the sum of the 20 ages, divided by 20.

The mean age is $\dfrac{(13 \times 9) + (14 \times 6) + (15 \times 3) + (16 \times 2)}{20} = \dfrac{278}{20} = 278 \div 20 = 13.9$ years.

d The range is the oldest – the youngest = 16 – 13 = 3 years.

Practice questions

1   Work out the **median** of each set of numbers.

a 12, 14, 18, 22, 30, 42   _____

b 3, 3, 4, 5, 5, 6, 7, 8, 8, 8 _____

c 2.6, 2.8, 4.4, 4.6, 5.0, 5.8, 7.5 _____

d 39, 40, 48, 57, 61, 65, 68, 82, 82, 85, 90 _____

e 14, 18, 18, 30, 60, 65, 70, 89 _____

2 Here are the weights of seven parcels.

2.4 kg   1.3 kg   1.0 kg   1.9 kg   1.8 kg   2.7 kg   1.7 kg

a Find the **median** and **range** of the weights.

Median _____ kg   Range _____ kg

b Why would you not use the mode as a measure of the average weight of the seven parcels?

_____.

3 Here are the weekly wages of five workers in a shop.

£100   £100   £100   £100   £600

a Work out the **mode**, the **median** and the **mean** wage.

Mode _____   Median _____   Mean _____

b Which is the best average to represent the wages? Give a reason. _____

_____.

4 The data in each question is displayed in a frequency table.

Find the **mode** and **range** for each set of data.

a

Number of days absent	0	1	2	3	4	5
Frequency	17	6	2	1	3	1

Mode _____   Range _____

b

Weight of cake (g)	38	39	40	41	42	43
Frequency	3	7	5	4	1	1

Mode _____   Range _____

6.2 Statistical diagrams

I can

- interpret different types of statistical diagrams

Example

This sectional percentage bar chart shows the ages of cars in two car parks.

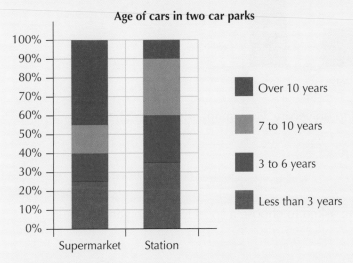

Age of cars in two car parks

Legend:
- Over 10 years
- 7 to 10 years
- 3 to 6 years
- Less than 3 years

a Which car park had a larger percentage of cars under 7 years old? Give a reason for your answer.

b What percentage of cars in the supermarket were over 10 years old?

c 20 cars in the station car park were over 10 years old. How many cars were in the car park altogether?

Solution

a 'Under 7' is the lower two sections of each column. This is higher for the station, so that car park had the larger percentage.

b This is the top section of the first bar. It goes from 55% to 100% so that is $100 - 55 = 45\%$.

c The top section of the station bar is 10% and this is 20 cars.

10% is $\frac{1}{10}$ of all the cars. There are $20 \times 10 = 200$ cars all together.

Practice questions

1 Here are the results of a survey of where 400 pupils are going when they leave school.

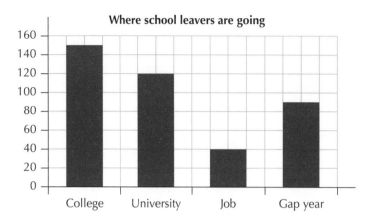

a More are going to college than to university. How many more? _____

b What percentage are starting a job? _____

2 The boys and girls in a school were asked to choose a sport to play in games lessons.

This chart shows their choices.

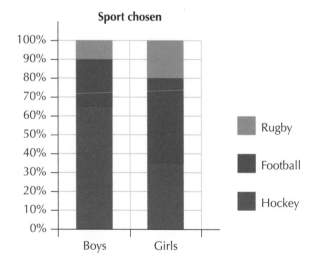

a Write down the most popular choice for girls _____

b What percentage of the boys chose football? _____

3 This pie chart shows the results of a survey of holiday destinations.

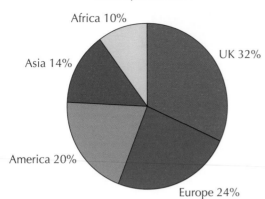

Holiday destinations

Africa 10%

Asia 14%

UK 32%

America 20%

Europe 24%

a What region was the mode? _____

b What fraction went to America? _____

c What percentage did not holiday in the UK? _____

   15 people in the survey went to Africa.

d How many went to America? _____

e How many people were in the survey? _____

4 This bar chart shows the medals won by four countries in the 2012 Olympic Games.

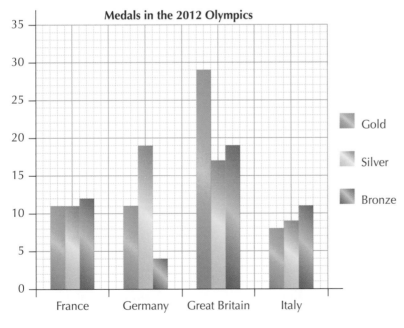

a Which country won most silver medals? _____

b Which country won fewest bronze medals? _____

c Which country won the same number of gold and silver medals? _____

d Which country won fewest medals overall? _____

5 This chart shows the population of the United Kingdom in 2012.

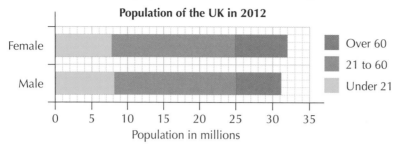

Population of the UK in 2012

- Over 60
- 21 to 60
- Under 21

Population in millions

a Estimate the number of females under 21. _____

b Estimate the number of females between 21 and 60. _____

c Estimate the total population of the UK. _____

d How do the distributions of the ages of men and women differ?

_____

_____

6 These pie charts show the grades achieved in the same exam in two schools.

Five grades, A to E, are possible.

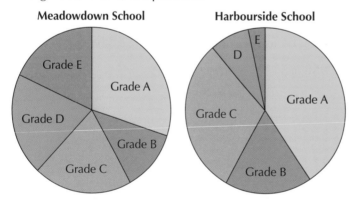

Meadowdown School   Harbourside School

Here are some statements. Say whether each one is True, False or Cannot Say.

Circle the correct answer.

a There were more A grades at Harbourside than
at Meadowdown.   True   False   Cannot Say

b The mode in Meadowdown was grade C.   True   False   Cannot Say

c More than 25% at Harbourside got grade C.   True   False   Cannot Say

d There were fewer Bs than As at Meadowdown   True   False   Cannot Say

e Meadowdown got more than twice as many Ds
as Harbourside.   True   False   Cannot Say

f Harbourside got a larger percentage of A and B grades   True   False   Cannot Say
than Meadowdown.

6.3 Line graphs

I can

- draw and interpret line graphs

Example

Adam is going for a long walk.

He walks for six hours and records how far he has travelled after each hour.

The results are shown in this line graph.

a How far does Adam walk altogether?

b How far does Adam walk in the second hour?

c How long does Adam take to walk 20 km?

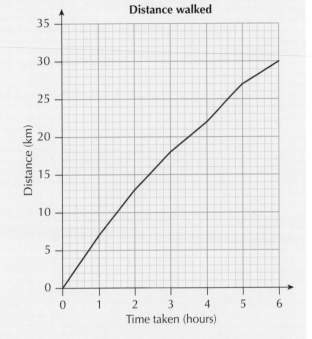

Solution

a He walks for six hours. The graph shows he has walked 30 km.

b The second hour is from time 1 hour to time 2 hours.

After 1 hour he has walked 7 km.

After 2 hours he has walked 13 km.

In the second hour he walked 13 − 7 = 6 km.

c Find 20 km on the vertical axis and go across horizontally to the curve. The point shows that he has walked for 3.5 hours.

Practice questions

1 The temperature in a garden was recorded every two hours from 08:00 until 20:00 and shown on this line graph.

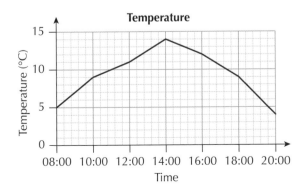

a Write down the temperature at 18:00. _____.

b Write down the highest recorded temperature. _____.

c Use the graph to estimate the time when the temperature first reached 7°C. _____.

2 Bamboo can grow very quickly.

The height of a bamboo was recorded at midday each day and is shown on this graph.

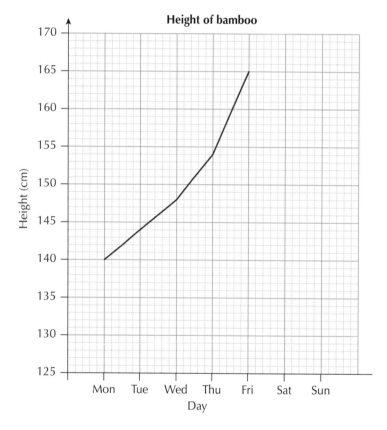

a What was the height at midday on Thursday? _____.

b On what day did the height first exceed 155 cm? _____.

c Work out the increase in height between midday Monday and midday Friday. _____.

d The height at midday on Saturday was 168 cm.

The height at midday on Sunday was 170 cm.

Extend the graph to show these values.

3 A car starts to move.

The speed is recorded every 10 seconds.

The values are shown on this graph.

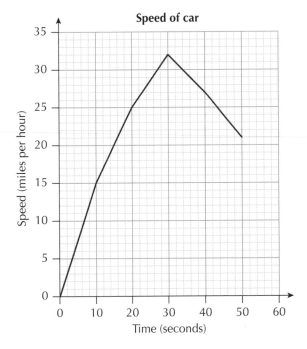

a Write down the speed after 10 seconds _____.

b What is the highest speed recorded? _____.

c After one minute the speed is 15 miles per hour. Extend the graph to show this.

4 This table shows the mass of a baby girl recorded every two months for a year.

Age (months)	0	2	4	6	8	10	12
Mass (kg)	3.2	5.2	6.4	7.4	8.0	8.5	8.9

a Use these axes to show the girl's mass on a line graph.

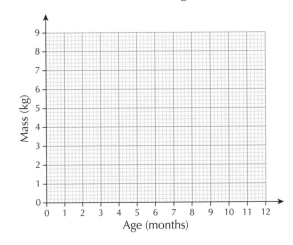

b Use your graph to estimate the girl's mass at

    i 3 months   _____   **ii** 11 months   _____

c Work out the increase in the mass of the girl

    i in the first 6 months   _____   **ii** in the second six months   _____

5   This line graph shows the distance travelled by a car on a three-hour journey.

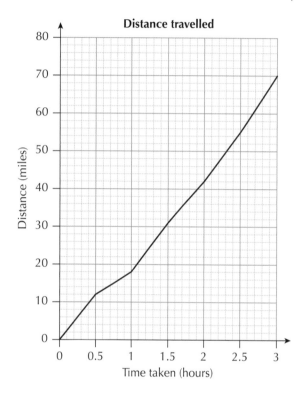

a How long did it take to travel 50 miles?   _____

b Did the car travel further in the first 1½ hours or the second 1½ hours? Justify your answer.

_____

_____

_____

Comments, next steps, misconceptions

Mental warm-up 1: Number

1 Multiply 3.6 by 100.

2 Divide 98 by 10.

3 Round 3.14159 to two decimal places.

4 Work out 40% of 30 people.

5 Work out 6 + −7.

6 Here is a multiplication: 22.5×29.2.
Which one of these is the correct answer?

65.7   240   657   2400   6570

7 Write down all the common factors of 12 and 18.

8 Work out the first three multiples of 20.

9 Write 800 m in kilometres.

10 Here is a sequence of numbers.

10   11   13   16   20   25

Work out the next number in the sequence.

11 Work out $\sqrt{81}$.

12 Write $\frac{36}{60}$ in its simplest form.

13 Which of these is the length of a spoon?

1.8 mm   18 mm   180 mm   1.8 cm

1.8 m

14 Work out the sixth square number.

15 Work out $2 + 3 \times 4$.

16 Work out $\sqrt[3]{125}$.

17 Write 600 mm in metres.

18 Which of these is a common multiple of 4 and 6?

30   40   50   60   70

19 Work out $8 - (3{-}5)$.

20 Work out the missing number here.

$43 \div 10 = \underline{\hspace{1cm}} \times 10$

Mental warm-up 2: Number/Algebra

1 Divide 4.5 by 100.

2 Work out the missing number.

$2.7 \times \underline{\hspace{1cm}} = 270$

3 Work out −10 −5.

4 Work out $\frac{5}{8}$ of 40 g.

5 Here are some numbers.

6   −5   4   −3   2

Find the smallest number in the list.

6 Work out the value of $3^2 + 4^2$.

7 Work out the value of 5^3.

8 Here are some fractions.

$\frac{2}{3}$ $\frac{3}{4}$ $\frac{5}{8}$

Work out which one is the largest?

9 Here is a sequence of numbers.

80   40   20   10   5   ____

Work out the next number.

10 Write down the coordinates of the point marked on this grid.

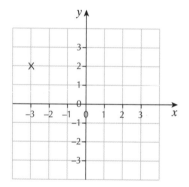

11 Here is a formula for the cost £c of n calls each month on a phone contract.

$c = 0.1n + 5$

Work out the value of c if $n = 35$.

12 Here is a formula. $p = 2a + 2b$

Work out the value of p if $a = 4.5$ and $b = 2.5$.

Mental warm-up 3: Ratio, proportion and rates of change/ Geometry and measures

1 Jason takes 15 minutes to complete a task and Alan takes 45 minutes.

Work out the ratio of the times. Write your answer as simply as possible.

2 How many lines of symmetry does a parallelogram have?

3 Work out the area of this shape.

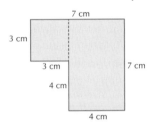

4 Work out the perimeter of the shape in Question 3.

5 Two angles of an isosceles triangle are equal to 25°. Work out the third angle.

6 All the angles round this point are the same size.

Work out the size of each one.

7 How many lines of symmetry does this shape have?

Mental warm-up 4: Probability/ Statistics

1 Each letter in this word is written on a separate card.

One card is chosen at random. Work out the probability that it is an A.

2 Work out the mean of these three lengths. 2 cm   6 cm   7 cm

3 Work out the median of these ages.

| 12 | 12 | 12 | 12 | 13 | 16 |
| 17 | 17 | 28 | 36 | 37 |

4 Here are twenty masses, in kilograms.

18	15	17	20	25	28
17	23	17	29	17	24
11	17	17	19	31	17
17	26

Work out the modal mass.

5 Work out the range of the masses in Question 4.

6

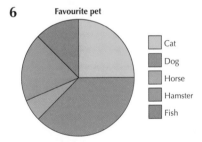

20 people voted for Cat. How many voted for Dog?

7 A dice is thrown. Work out the probability of throwing at least 3. Write your answer as simply as possible.

Record of achievement certificate

Step 3

Congratulations on achieving Step 3!

Name _____

Date _____

Signed _____